"I was so lucky to have such an inspiring ballet teacher like Dawn Crouch growing up. The wisdom that she shared has helped me to become a better dancer, but more importantly a better person."

Jadyn Dahlberg
Indiana University
Miami Ballet

"Miss Dawn allowed for ballet class to be a haven for artistic expression. As I now teach young students ballet, I hope to instill the same confidence and artistry that Miss Dawn cultivated in me."

Hannah Box
University of South Florida
Patel Conservatory - Tampa, FL

"Mrs Crouch's training reflects in my performance and teaching career."

Madison Grace Lynn
Savannah Ballet

BALLET HELPS EVERYTHING!

A Garage Ballet Book

DAWN C CROUCH

based on a true story.

Many Thanks and Much Love to All My Students and Especially My Two Daughters
Dominique and Caroline

INTRODUCTION

Ballet Helps Everything! - Ten Reasons Why

"I don't keep my secrets or my knowledge to myself." – Natalia Makarova

Today, students enjoy many choices – soccer, skiing, ice skating, basketball, swimming, lacrosse, tennis, volleyball, track and field, golf, gymnastics, martial arts, on and on.

So little time, so many choices.

Why Ballet?

Nutcracker Season is over by mid to late December. End of the year Recital is months away at that point then... Summer looms like a big black hole in the training galaxy.

Why should you motivate yourself, your child, and your students to pursue their study of ballet as a year-round activity?

Why are the consistent, ongoing goals demonstrated in the study of ballet important to their lives?

I have an answer that is both simple and complex.

Ballet helps everything!

There it is...

The old adage that I've heard ancient teachers, young teachers, aspiring students, company members, and world-famous dancers say time and again.

Ballet helps everything!

Ballet supports a global culture and a common language that makes it possible for a student of ballet to travel to any city or country in the world, and be able to fully understand and participate in class.

A centuries old art form with a codified series of steps, ballet delivers a specialized yet universal skillset better than any other physical training platform.

What does that mean? And is it really true?

My first dance lessons were taught in New Orleans by a teacher with fire dyed red hair. The studio, converted from half of a small grocery store, was on Downman Road down from the Danziger Bridge and next to the Intercoastal Canal.

I studied ballet, tap, jazz, and acrobatics – all in a one-hour class! Most of our time was spent changing shoes. But I was pretty good at the dance part of things, compared to the other kids. My teacher gave me gold stars pasted on an index card and proclaimed that I had talent.

After my last "number" in that revue, I remember sitting with the audience in a frou-frou fluffy net costume beside my Mom to watch the rest of the show. Please, I know and beg forgiveness from the Ballet gods for this terrible breach of etiquette... A huge faux pas for any student to wear a costume in the auditorium!

But I vividly remember being mesmerized by a girl dancing a solo in orange pointe shoes that had little taps on the pointe. Toe-tap! She looked just like one of the hippos in Disney's Fantasia and I thought she was terrific!!

My smile was ear to ear, and my mother quickly pointed out that the gums above my teeth were showing. Undeterred, I pushed my lip down with my index finger and continued to be enthralled by the girl's bulbous performance.

I turned to look at my mother, who was a lookalike for Vivian Leigh of Scarlett O'Hara fame and a former dancer/acrobat who performed in USO shows when she was young, and loudly proclaimed, "I want to dance like that."

My simple innocent, heartfelt statement had far reaching ramifications.

My mother was horrified.

She grabbed me by the elastic straps on my frou-frou costume and hauled me out of the theatre, right then and there. I did not even get to see the end of the toe-tap dance.

Too bad... So sad.

The very next day, mom rousted me out of bed to enroll me in a new dance school – a school devoted exclusively to the study of ballet.

Any ballet dancer from New Orleans in the last century took class from Leila Haller, my teacher and the grand dame of ballet in the city. To name a few: Royse Fernandez, Kirk Peterson, Joseph Giacobbe, Harvey Hysell, Karen Pedersen Schaffenburg, Barbara Pontecorvo, and Jerel Hilding!

Miss Haller was the first American to dance with Paris Opera Ballet in the early 1920s. She studied with the originals, the classic teachers who are now officially legend - August Bourneville, Albert Aveline, Nicolas Legate, and Enrico Cecchetti himself.

When she retired as a dancer and returned to the States, Balanchine invited her to relocate to New York and teach at his newly formed School of American Ballet. She declined. In 1928, Miss Haller founded the ballet school bearing her name in the Crescent City.

At the time I took my first class with Miss Haller, she was in her eighties, and stood ramrod straight in the front right corner of the square room with a warped wooden floor that served as our studio.

In the non-air-conditioned, New Orleans heat and humidity which is often compared to a sub-tropical jungle, Miss Haller stood dressed in black tights, a turtleneck leotard and a grey wool skirt.

She did not give class. She commanded it.

Miss Haller placed me in her Advanced Intermediate class, which I immediately thought was a mistake.

My former flame headed teacher had put me on pointe just before the debacle recital. At eleven years old, I was already tall, and she needed me to fill out a line and dance with the older girls.

Of course, that is never a good reason to put anyone on pointe! It's a horrible reason! But what's done is hard to undo sometimes...

I remember walking to the wooden barre directly across from the mirrors at the very front of the class. A small group of prim, ballet snob girls converged and informed me that I was in their place at the barre.

I danced holding onto a steel handle near the back door for several years.

When I put pointe shoes on my feet that day, they felt as if they were made of solid concrete. I was in mortal pain and I had no idea how to even tie the ribbons. My former teacher had us use elastic garter straps to keep the shoes in place. Ha! So, what was I going to do with a good eighteen to twenty inches of ribbon?

I crisscrossed the pretty in pink ribbons in back of my Achilles then again in front before tying the remaining ribbon into a neat bow just above the middle of my ankle.

Though most of the students were as friendly as piranhas, a very charitable, older girl, one of the best in the class, took me to the side and gently said, "That's not how it's done."

Seriously!!!

She showed me how to tie my pointe shoe ribbons, inside ribbon crosses over outside ribbon then again in back. Keep the ribbon as flat as possible, tie a knot, then tuck the knot under the ribbon in the hollow at the inside of the ankle. NEVER- over or on top of the Achilles tendon.

Sometime later, this same dancer showed me how to sew the ends of my ribbons so the ends wouldn't fall out or even possibly come untied during a performance. Her lessons offered all the essentials of ribbon tying related to pointe work!

The rest of the class continued to dance indignantly around us. The other students glared then acted as if I was a ghost who didn't really exist and should be roundly ignored.

After my shoes were tied correctly, I took hold of the barre and executed one single Échappé, finishing in a tight fifth position before...

Hobbling off to the dressing room.

I did return wearing soft leather ballet shoes and finish the class, but I was treated like a leper. No one wanted to get too close. They might catch something.

At the end of class, Miss Haller, looking down her straight little nose at me, commented that she was having a meeting of company members at her home after class. Would I like to join her? The rest of the dancers were aghast because her simple statement put me on par with them, even if I did have make up work to do.

I did not deserve this... My teacher's faith gave me the confidence that eventually led to performance.

Miss Haller remains my most beloved teacher and mentor. She taught ballet technique handed down directly from the masters, and I eventually became a teacher at her school, kind of like Jane Eyre. I was tapped to help her open a second location in the city a year before I married and moved to Houston to dance with Houston Ballet.

A good portion of my life has been spent within the four walls of a ballet studio, whether in class, rehearsal, or onstage.

THREE KEYS SUPPORT THE TEN REASONS

"Someone need not be perfect to be a great dancer – feeling a soul is more important than what the body can do." - Marcia Haydée

Balance, Posture, and Body Alignment form the basis of all ballet training. These Three Keys will improve physical proficiency and assist any type of movement attempted by a human body.

Posture is how a person holds their body when standing or sitting, so a person deals with posture throughout their entire life. Training your body's posture begins when you are very young, for good or bad.

Have you ever noticed an older person with humped shoulders who just cannot straighten up to save themselves? Yes, that condition may be genetic, or a result of osteoporosis or some other medical condition, but the habits of poor posture begin at an early age.

Bent, rounded shoulders may get a start from sitting poorly in school. Maybe the student uses their desk as a bed and develops a habit of slouching all over everything whenever they sit down, at a computer station, watching TV, while eating, in the car. It's easy to slouch, and slouch, and slouch even more as the day progresses.

Your body will assume a posture. Whether a good posture or a bad one, it is your choice. The exercises taught in ballet class develop a carriage and bearing that conveys a confident self-image.

Good posture, as in bearing or position, has parallels to activities other than sports. The ability to hold and play an instrument in orchestra or band often depends on good posture.

Good posture even staves off osteoporosis by presenting your body with a viable reason to maintain the calcium needed for strong bone structure. If you don't use it, you lose it.

I think of two stories when I consider a person's posture. One is a game my brother used to play when we were young called "The Man with No Bones." The object was to act as if all the bones in your body evaporated – a terrifying thought – and to be as loose and malleable as possible which leads to my second example...

Sometimes in front of car washes or fast food restaurants, the proprietor places a bendy stick of a blow up with arms and fringed hair that deflates and inflates to help catch customers attention.

One minute the stick figure is inflated and standing up straight and tall; the next minute the blower turns off momentarily and the stick structure collapses in on itself. That's what someone with poor posture reminds me of... a deflating stick figure with no control that crumples in on itself.

A Person with no Strength to Maintain a Decent Posture is a Person with No Bones.

Balance is the even distribution of weight that enables someone or something to remain upright and steady.

Ballet is all about combining a series of steps or movements that require an advanced degree of balance to execute. When you dance, you are always anticipating and moving toward the next step in the combination.

Sports and other physical activities, as well as mental activities – Have you ever heard of Chess or Shogi? – all demand a plan or strategy that results in forward motion, and movement tempered by balance.

Offense must be supported by defense.

The moves a player makes may change direction, stop, or start suddenly. The smooth delivery of physical activity or mental exercise means the weight of your body or the depth of your thought must be anticipatory and pro-active to achieve success.

Body Alignment is closely related to Posture but more specifically, involves the placement of shoulders and hips.

Think of body alignment like a car's headlights. If you are driving down the street on a particularly dark night, you want your headlights to be aimed on the road in front of you not to the side of the road or up into the trees. Right?

Body alignment is much the same. Are your shoulders and hips aimed ahead of you? Are you pointed in the right direction?

Mastering the Three Keys of Ballet improves poise and control over every aspect of your body's movement and supports all additional reasons why Ballet Helps Everything!

But how, and why does ballet benefit a student?

And by ballet, I do mean ballet, the specific name brand three hundred-year-old plus discipline. I don't mean just any generic form of dance, or free dance, or let's get in front of the television and rag it out dance. I love moving around and free expression but...

I am talking about the organized, collected, and collated series of steps that progressed from Renaissance Italian nobility to the courts of Louis XIV (1638-1715), Le Roi Soleil.

The Sun King himself gathered steps and styles of movement from folk dancing and sports of the period to create what we now recognize as an incredible art form.

Ballet also employs the unique principle of turnout. Instead of standing with your leg and foot facing straight forward, ballet encourages rotation of the leg in the ball and socket joint of the hips which causes the knee and foot to turn outward, away from the center of the body. Dancers must work to develop the strength to hold the rotation of the leg in place.

Turnout is a hallmark of ballet technique and accomplishes two important missions.

The first is stability. When a dancer stands on one leg, the stability of the body increases if the balance uses a "turned-out" position.

The second reason is extension. A dancer is able to lift their leg much higher in front, on the side, and back in an arabesque if the leg is turned out. Extensions of professional dancers often are high over their head. The physical structure of the hip gets in the way if a dancer raises their leg in a "turned in" position, limiting the height to a ninety degree extension which is only hip high.

I know what you're saying.

"Well, that's great and everything, but I'm not going to be a professional ballet dancer. I'm too old, too young, too short, tall, too something else, fill in the blank, to do anything like that."

Or... "My child can't stay still for two minutes, or I can't get them off the sofa, or fill in the blank. How the heck does any of this apply to me or my child?"

But that's the most important part of the secret.

The ten reasons why Ballet Helps Everything can be directly applied to everyone who studies ballet in any way, shape, or form, whether you begin as an adult or a child.

The benefits have nothing to do with perfection and everything to do with confidence.

Ballet helps you enjoy the body that you live in, day in, day out, and so much more.

Ballet elevates your game no matter what game you're playing by improving your body's functionality. Ballet even contributes to your increased longevity.

Think of ballet as a vault that contains priceless treasures.

The Bolshoi Ballet, founded in 1776, is one of the oldest and most acclaimed ballet companies in the world. How do you think the original members of the ballet company were chosen?

Do you think the founders had auditions all over Russia and brought together the best, brightest, most promising physical specimens of children to form what has become a jewel in the cultural crown of Russian legacy?

No. Not even close.

Before the Bolshoi was a famous ballet company, it was an orphanage. The dancers in the first company were random children with no family, no special talents, and no known aptitude for physical prowess.

They were children who were employed by the Prince as dancers during the fall and winter and used as field hands to plant, cultivate, and harvest crops in the spring and summer. The art of ballet molded them into the first dancers of a tradition that made history.

CHAPTER ONE

SPATIAL AWARENESS

*"If you don't know where you're going, you might wind up someplace else." – Yogi
Berra*

THE ABILITY TO see and understand the relationship of two or more
objects – animate or inanimate – to each other and to your own body
in terms of space and distance is known as Spatial Awareness.

This ability implies an understanding of your location in reference
to objects and people near you. Spatial Awareness is important because
it establishes the concepts of direction, distance and place.

Easy? Right... Let me present an example.

Have you ever been in a grocery store at Christmas time when the
skinny little aisles are crowded with other shoppers? Picture someone
perusing a display rack for an esoteric item that is not easily found.

The person doesn't have to be elderly or have three children playing and climbing all over the shopping cart. Just an average person of an average age during rush hour at the grocery.

Their buggy may be parked discreetly to the side, but somehow, they stand smack dab in the middle of the aisle searching for the item on their list.

No one can get around them, and they are completely oblivious. They have no freaking idea where they are, or what they're doing, or that they are causing a monumental logjam in the aisle.

This is an example of a lack of spatial awareness.

Spatial Awareness simply means that you as a person know where your body begins and ends, and also where your body stands in relation to everyone and everything around it.

Sounds so simple. But remember our heedless shopper.

The study of ballet teaches the life skill of Spatial Awareness in abundance.

On a performance level, consider the Corps de Ballet, that is all the background dancers who act and create the scene for the principal dancers. Their movements are synchronized in step, not only with the music, but with each other. They move as one body, hence the term Corps de Ballet which means Body of the Ballet.

Would *Swan Lake* or *Giselle* be the same without those background dancers?

No.

The Corp de Ballet's contribution to the aesthetic of the ballet experience is heartbreakingly real, even if the dancers' names are usually not listed on the marquee.

The connection between the dancers in the corps is carefully encouraged and realized through the long hours of rehearsal leading up to the performance.

These dancers are aware of their placement on the stage, the line of their orchestrated steps, the height of the extension of their legs and arms standardized.

They practice where to look, the position of their head, and the intricate patterns of the choreography.

Dancers notice all the details. They are observant and possess high memorization abilities. That's why dancers make great spies!! Think of

Red Sparrow and the ballet dancer in *John Wick 3* who will be featured in the next installment of that popular Keanu Reeves franchise. There's a reason that's so believable!

Think of real life examples: Mata Hari and Josephine Baker. Wait! They were known for erotic and jazz dance but guess what? They also trained in ballet.

How exactly does ballet help you develop spatial awareness?

When you are dancing in class, you must pay attention to other dancers around you, to the space or lack of space between you and others.

This is one reason I recommend formalized classes with several students over private lessons.

In addition, private lessons can become a frustrating tug of war as the teacher tries to cajole their single solitary student to keep moving. With the spotlight on a single student, there is a tendency to act like a deer in the headlights and the student moves less as the class drags on.

The only exception?

Individual coaching for a particular part or role is an absolute necessity. When you are rehearsing a solo variation for a performance, you deserve your one on one time with your teacher.

But in regular ballet classes, a camaraderie and - let's be honest - a little healthy competition, builds as all the students work together. Everyone is tired, sweaty. Everyone is working as hard as they can or at least, they should be.

Grand Pas de Quatre was a ballet divertissement, i.e., a short dance, that was first presented in London on July 12, 1845.

The ballet caused a complete sensation, but not because of the music or choreography. It was acclaimed because the four greatest ballerinas of the time, Lucile Grahn, Carlotta Grisi, Fanny Cerrito, and Marie Taglioni, danced on stage at the same time.

The professional rivalry between the dancers was explored and exhibited throughout the piece, which included an opening, four variations, and a finale.

Each variation in the divertissement was choreographed to display the individual strengths of the showcased dancer. The piece was a huge success that fortunately did not devolve into a cat fight. Grand Pas de Quatre is still performed today by competing ballerinas. Fun to watch!

The movement and structure of the ballet class creates a special energy, a good driving synergy that everyone in the class can feed from.

Dancing in an organized class encourages and supports a student because the success and failings of other dancers are visible and offer a chance to learn and absorb.

In fact, it's always great to "dance up" in class.

Don't know what I mean? Let me explain.

When you "dance up," this means that some people in your class are better dancers than you are. Applaud!! You are being presented a golden opportunity because those dancers will motivate you to try harder.

Learn from them. Copy their movement, how they approach and perform a step.

What if you're the best in the class?

Then you have an additional obligation.

Other dancers look up to you, and it is important for you to dance your best and be a good example for everyone in the class. Always.

"I don't go to a gym; I don't do yoga. I don't do personal training." - Mikhail Baryshnikov

There is a structure that is integral to the traditional ballet class. Students begin the class at the barre, where they perform a series of exercises designed to warm-up, condition, and strengthen every joint and muscle in the body.

After the barre work is complete, the class moves away from the barre to the middle of the room, where they will perform the steps and combinations known as Centre.

Before any Centre work begins, the students first stand in parallel lines, equidistant from each other, with each dancer in the back row occupying the space or "window" between the two dancers in the line in front of them.

Practically, the dancers do this so they can better see themselves in the mirror and judge their own movement.

Remember that you are always your best teacher.

Ballet is as much about learning to correct yourself as accepting corrections from your instructor. But the bottom line is that before any steps or exercises begin in the center, the spatial ordering of each student in the class is observed and adjusted.

During Centre work, dancers move diagonally across the floor, sometimes from the back of the room to the front, sometimes from the front to the back. They perform steps side to side, front to back, and must understand the concept of "your corner" as opposed to always facing "the corner."

All the while, the dancers need to know where they are, where their body is facing, and where they're going next.

Center work solidifies the lessons of spacing. The dancers must be competent in this skill, or the class will be a train wreck.

Body alignment, one of the three keys of ballet, assists in the development of spatial awareness.

Body alignment is essential because it directs the position of a dancer's shoulders and hips. Body alignment sets the line of motion.

If while riding a horse, an activity which makes me very nervous indeed, you look down at the saddle, check your feet in the stirrups, or look around wondering if your mom, or boyfriend, or whoever, is watching, then the horse will go wherever the horse wants to go. Why? Because you are not steering the horse. The horse is steering itself.

You must look between the horse's ears. Through your body language and the awareness of the space you are working within, you should be the one directing the horse where to go... Not the other way around.

Or try driving a car while texting. Don't do this. Repeat... DO NOT DO THIS EVER!! If you do, then you are not looking where you're going. It's as if you've given the car permission to drive itself. NOT!

In class, your shoulders and hips should face the direction where you want to go. You will be asked to maneuver and perform steps that cover the entire expanse of the studio from one wall of to the opposite, usually while other groups of people are simultaneously moving as well.

You will go forward, back, diagonally, while turning and/or jumping. I think it's pretty important to know where the next person is located.

Don't you? Absolutely!

You must be aware of your place in the room, and everyone else's position, or you will bowl somebody over. Simple as that!

I was in class with on a regular basis with a male dancer who just was not very spatially aware. When he got going, you had to watch out. He would completely knock into you and push you down, when he didn't mean to. He wasn't trying to be nasty or anything, but at the same time, he really didn't have a clue where he was.

Once onstage, he turned left to do a sauté as I turned right to dance the same step. We managed to avoid each other but my mother, sitting in the audience, said she heard me tell him in no uncertain terms, "The other way. Go the other way!!"

When you train to be aware of your surroundings, you will cultivate a better grasp of what's going on in those surroundings. You will perceive a problem, a need, or an opportunity, and be able to respond quickly.

Perhaps when hosting a party, looking for an apartment, or even ministering to your children. You will be responsive and ready to act.

Ballet helps you to be mindful of people moving around you. That can lead to good breaks and opportunities, but it can also alert you to possible danger as well.

When I became a student of Miss Haller, there was one big glitch. Miss Haller's studio, the only ballet school in New Orleans at the time, was located at the far side of the Garden District on Jeannette Street between Broadway and Carroll-

ton. It was quite a long distance from my home in East Gentilly. One and a half hour travel time, one way.

Mothers did not drop off and pick up students from class as they commonly do today. My mother informed me that I would be taking the public service bus to and from class. Period. The end.

Now I know you're probably thinking... That was a different time. Life was safer. People looked out for other people.

I assure you that New Orleans has never been a particularly safe city, especially when you're a young girl on a public transit bus, alone at night.

The city is full of magical characters and scenes that are unique and timeless. A great place to visit. A lot of fun. People are really hospitable and super nice, but there's always been a dangerous element to New Orleans.

You have to watch your back, like in any big city. There are areas that are worse. There are areas that are better, but when you're taking one public service bus for an hour, then you have to change to another bus for another half hour ride, you better know what's happening around you.

My aptitude for spatial awareness learned in my ballet classes, was essential to me on those rides. One incident stands out: An alleged criminal rushed onto the bus chased by the NOPD Police... with their guns drawn.

Now, I could have frozen in place. I could have just sat there but... I took cover.

I was able to overcome my fight and flight response and move out of the way by crawling under the seat. It was the right move because the suspect being chased pulled other passengers from their plastic molded turquoise seats into the narrow aisle for the police to trip over.

The suspect eventually kicked a window out in the back of the bus and escaped. The cops followed him. I, and my fellow passengers, helped the unfortunates who were used as blockades. No one was seriously injured.

Thank the Lord that the cops didn't fire their guns, but the suspect wasn't going to go searching under a seat for a passenger either.

I'd like to say that is the only dangerous situation I've ever been in, but that would not be the truth.

Being spatially aware really does prepare you for the unexpected that can occur in your everyday life. That's always a big plus.

. . .

A healthy "City Awareness" in an essential defensive tool in almost any environment.

If you notice a danger, whether in the guise of a person or situation, it's much easier to steer clear than deal with confrontation.

If you heed warnings in the form of a suspicious individual, setting, or even a threatening natural disaster such as a hurricane, tornado, or fire, then you will be better prepared.

If you recognize what is happening around you, understand where your body is, realize what your body can do, and tell your body how to move within that environment, you have a much better chance of survival.

Just reflecting on the basics!!

"But," you say, "Isn't that something that just happens? Aren't people aware of their surroundings as a matter of course?"

You have a point.

Some people are innately aware of where their body is at any given moment. That person might have been born with good reflexes and a great reaction time.

However, most of us need additional training to discover how to relate to inanimate objects and other people around us, moving cars, opening streetcar doors, escalators, things that we encounter in the outside world, our day-to-day environment.

CHAPTER TWO

FLEXIBILITY

"Flexibility is the key to Stability."
- John Wooden

FLEXIBILITY REFERS to a property of an animate or inanimate object that is capable of being bent or is pliable, but it also means being responsive to change and adaptable to shifts in a situation or the environment.

Notice the two separate definitions.

You might think that the first definition is the only one that ballet teaches, but you'd be wrong. The first definition has a direct bearing on the physical stretching and building of muscle memory.

When a dancer takes class or is onstage during a performance, flexibility also implies being mentally adaptable and responsive to change.

If need be, adjustments and corrections in position or placement can be flawlessly executed.

Flexibility is important to the body because it keeps your muscles supple, moving. Flexibility helps build strength, endurance, stamina and the innate ability to cope with surprises that happen to come your way, whether an accidental fall or a quick change in your body's position or stance.

You might be going in one direction and somebody calls out to you, so you turn quickly toward another direction.

If your body is not very flexible, you can literally wrench a joint, or tear a muscle doing something like that.

How many times are we going in several directions at once? I'm willing to bet quite a few. Our lives move quickly, and so do we.

Ballet maximizes flexibility and muscles will be in better shape and able to adapt.

What if something as simple as a misstep causes a fall?

Flexibility can help you be able to fall better, and hopefully incur less injury than someone who is stiff and rigid. There are tons of ordinary examples in walking, running or any other physical sport. Flexibility guards against injury.

Here is an example taken from medical literature, a terrible example but true. Sometimes when a person driving a car sees an impending crash, perhaps another car pulls out in front of them, and there's nothing they can do and no way to avoid the crash, that person can actually tense their muscles so much that bones are broken and muscles torn, simply because of the intense tension, and lack of flexibility in those muscles. There's no give.

Flexibility is vital to the body's ability to move and adapt to normal and emergent situations that occur during regular daily activities.

The stretchy kind of flexibility can be naturally occurring. Some students inherit muscles as supple as wet spaghetti. Super flexible. They are able to do splits in every direction - front, back, and side - as well as backbends and Y-scales. Easy Peasy!

I admit that this type of flexibility has a certain appeal to it. But hyper flexibility can often make for a weak dancer who is prone to injury because the body is so difficult to control.

This type of dancer faces a lifetime of work on strengthening techniques. Flexibility may be their best talent but can also become their greatest liability if not tamed by strength and control.

Most of us just are not that flexible. We really can't do splits then perform a scorpion, holding your foot and pulling it up in a curved arabesque above your head while continuing to stand on one foot and at the same time, munch a peanut butter sandwich.

Most of us really can't do that... to start with.

Many dancers might not be able to do that to end with either, but flexibility is a skill that will improve with work and practice. Whether your shoulders, hips, feet, legs, or back, the flexibility of muscles and joints will gradually increase with daily, consistent stretching exercises.

Flexibility also enables a dancer to move with an increased fluidity that enhances the quality of motion.

Many times, dancers are pictured as being rigid and stiff. Think of the typical ballet snob stereotype. Someone who moves like an automaton with their nose stuck up in the air.

If this is the type of dancer that you notice at the studio you visit or are taking classes from, consider changing studios. This is NOT the standard you want to emulate.

Ballet training should enhance movement not stymie it. The dancer should appear fluid and smooth as they perform, and not jerk or run from one pose to another. Seek a studio that encourages, rather than suppresses movement of the human body.

An aside... I'm always wary of studios that ask Pre-Ballet students to stand on plastic dots placed on the floor. A good ballet teacher should not need this type of crutch to control the behavior of their students. Studios like this generally teach their students to pose, not dance.

An Example... I had the privilege of dancing for the New Orleans Opera Ballet when I was fourteen which is young to be a paid union card carrying dancer! The audition for the parts was strenuous and demanding. We were asked to jump, turn, do combinations across the floor.

There was one solo part.

When it came time to audition for that role, the director asked us to walk across the floor.

That was the audition.

My friends and I did our best ballet walk from the upstage corner of the huge studio diagonally to the downstage corner. Our arms did not bounce, but remained steady yet fluid. We walked toe to heel through a perfect first position. Our heads were tilted toward the audience, and our walk was smooth although our hips and shoulders were unmoving, stilted, and more than a little stiff.

One of the girls was a little older than us, eighteen as I remember, and she alone understood what the director was looking for.

She started at the corner and walked with her hips not her feet driving the forward motion. Her arms curled and looped, as sensuous as snakes.

Her head dipped and wound around her neck. She demanded the attention of everyone in the room.

She walked like a woman, and we walked like prim little girls.

We were technically better dancers, certainly as flexible but not nearly as fluid as this girl.

Guess who got the solo part?

Stretching exercises done on a regular basis promotes elasticity and shapes muscle memory.

Properly warmed up and stretched muscles are not going to grab, go into spasm, or react in a way that will hurt the dancer.

Improved flexibility will strengthen the muscles that are being stretched by building "muscle memory," the ability to repeat a specific movement with improved efficiency and accuracy, acquired through practice and repetition.

An important part of learning and practicing actual steps, muscle memory is also fundamental to properly stretching.

Think of your muscles as a giant set of fibrous rubber bands. If you gradually extend the range of a rubber band, then it may be possible to coax the material to expand but... If you jerk or overstretch a rubber band onto a bundle that is too big, then it is far more likely to snap.

The primary aim of stretching exercises should be to slowly and progressively lengthen the stretch of the muscle fibers to their greatest range of extension. Your body knows when you've reached maximum stretch. Your muscles will yell, "That's enough for now!"

Hold all stretches for a full eight counts, or until your muscles begin to relax into the stretch.

Yes.

The feeling or sense of impending pain subsides, and your muscles ease into the extension. Then repeat the stretch... usually a minimum of four times during your session.

The initial stretch followed by the feeling of tightness, then easing is how muscle memory is built.

Over a period of time, your muscles will become comfortable with the first extension, and you will be able to push a little more, stretch a little harder.

Gradually, and a little at a time. Two Cautions...

Whether a dancer is super flexible like cooked spaghetti, or not, never engage in "ballistic" stretching. That is, the bouncy, bouncy, bouncy, sharp sudden pushes into a stretch that I often see runners on the side of the road doing.

Ballistic stretching can cause a great deal of harm. Think of piano or guitar strings snapping and breaking.

That is what happens during this type of violent stretching. You are injuring your muscles. Never stretch like this. The beneficial effects of stretching are lost, and the result is useless.

Second pet peeve... Personally, I do not like anyone "helping" me to stretch by grabbing my leg, shoulder, foot and forcefully pushing my muscles beyond my limits.

I have heard people say that stretching with a partner can be helpful, and my retort is that it can be helpful only if your partner proceeds with great caution and knows you well.

Ultimately, that person cannot feel the impulses that define the limit of your muscles on a particular day and in a particular stretch.

I've seen more injuries from ballistic stretching and well-meaning partners pushing a person beyond their body's limitations than anything else having to do with stretching.

Injuries precipitated by careless, ill-advised stretching tend to linger... for months and possibly even years.

Once muscle fiber is torn, and make no mistake, that's what happens when tissue is stretched beyond endurance, the fibers must heal, but will never be the same.

In a flash, all benefits from stretching are lost.

Read that again and remember it because it's true.

CHAPTER THREE

STRENGTH AND STAMINA

"Push harder than yesterday if you want a different tomorrow."

NOT EXACTLY SURE who said this first, and I did look it up, but the quote sums up the concept of working hard to achieve the results you desire.

Strength and Stamina can be defined as the capacity of the body and mind to sustain prolonged stressful effort or activity.

Strength and stamina refer to building a person's endurance.

Notice that the definitions of the Ballet Helps Everything! reasons often have meanings that are twofold, with one definition referring to physical qualities, and one pertaining to mental capacity and character.

Both are equally important to you as a dancer, and as a person.

Strength is very much like the virtue of courage. Strength often makes everything else possible.

A person can be spatially aware, flexible, and possess a host of other talents but what if that person is weak?

They will not be able to perform, and the goal of ballet always sets the aim of finding the balance between a student's potential and performance. Sometimes they don't mix very well. A student may have great potential, but if they don't come to class regularly, don't apply the lessons they learn, and don't think they can... Then they can't.

That is a phrase that I do not allow a student to utter in class because if they do, then they are doomed. A student will never perform the step if they think they can't do it.

"The only way to do it is to do it."
- Merce Cunningham

When I was a very young teacher, I taught twenty-two classes a week, in addition to my own classes as a ballet student and a course load of fifteen academic hours at the University of New Orleans. Ballet financed my college education. I paid my tuition by dancing and teaching.

I was given mostly Pre-Ballet and Adult Basic Ballet classes to teach, and I remember being very intimidated by my adult students.

At the time, I was nineteen years old, yet I was the teacher. There was one person in particular who terrified me, a physics professor at Tulane who had decided that she really wanted to study ballet.

One morning, I remember she was very upset to the point that I stopped the class. She was flustered, red in the face, and on the verge of tears.

I walked up to her and asked, "What's wrong? What are you thinking? What can I do to help you?"

She looked up and replied through gritted teeth, "I understand this. I logically know what it is you want me to do, but somehow, I cannot connect what I want my body to do with what my body is doing. I cannot make this happen."

I calmed her down by saying, "Let's just do small steps at a time. Let's pick one thing to work on this week. Next week, we'll work on something else."

My words seemed to soothe her mixture of anger and panic, but her concern speaks to problems encountered by dancers who begin their study as adults, as well as younger students whose skills advance like broken gears in jumps and starts, rather than a smooth progression.

. . .

Impatience is rampant.

Many adult dancers and often middle school dancers who are just starting pointe work, expect instant results. They tend to want short-cuts, and think that their experience as skiers, runners, swimmers, ice skaters, their chosen sport, etc., will help their study of ballet.

Nothing could be farther from the truth. While ballet helps everything, very few sports training programs translate to expertise in ballet.

The defeatist attitude is often summed up in the simple phrase, "I can't do that."

Don't put limitations or blinders on your ability to progress. Be open. Be positive.

How many times do we stop ourselves, or put limits on our own abilities, because we will not even try something new, or work to master a skill at any level? That's just such a self-limiting way to live.

Is that what you want? Do you want to just stop yourself? "Oh, I would go travel, but I can't." Well, that just killed that!

Or "I would, but it's too much trouble."

Or, any number of self-limiting things that we say to ourselves, that stop us cold. It's not even because another person makes you stop. You do it to yourself...

Ballet teaches you that you don't master something in a day, but with a persistent attitude, you will get better and improve.

I've seen people return to class after being injured in car wrecks and rehabilitate their ability to move. Cultivate an attitude of persistence that will allow you to become stronger.

I remember another adult student who told me that she could not complete the barre because she couldn't sweat.

I know anyone who's taken ballet class out there will laugh when I tell them that, because it's almost impossible to take a ballet class and not break a sweat.

If you do happen to be in a ballet class and you're not breaking a sweat, then you need to look for another teacher or studio.

You need to work to a point where your cardiovascular system gets revved up, and yes, to the point that you're going to sweat, whether you say you can or not.

I posed a question to her: Why was she taking ballet class?

Once I convinced her that she could and indeed would sweat, and that it was a good cleansing thing, she became quite the dancer, but we had to hurdle that limitation first.

"I can't do it!" Where do people get stuff like that? Why do they believe it?

Potential vs. Performance is a balancing act that begins in Pre-Ballet. I love teaching the 3-5 year old students. They try everything. They NEVER say they can't do it. And when they make a mistake, they laugh heartily and are still young enough to be cute and funny.

Parents of Pre-Ballet watch enraptured by the potential that their young dancer represents. The promise of every small movement or mastery is magnified.

Then something happens...

The Pre-Ballet student grows and enters basic class, and the parents who filmed every rehearsal suddenly see that training is a process that requires small triumphs and the passage of time to achieve results.

The performance of a Basic level dancer is never as hopeful or polished when compared to the potential of Pre-Ballet.

Parents - and I don't just mean Moms - often point out their child's deficiencies to me. They ask, in a rather condescending and irritated voice, whether I have noticed their student's bent knees, protruding stomach, or gangly arms?

Now, I am a person that has trained and studied ballet for most of my life. I started my dance training when I was three; switched to a ballet only studio when I was eleven; put myself through college teaching over twenty ballet classes a week; danced professionally; and have taught without a break since.

I am the person who tells Sugar Plum or Swan Queen that she is sitting in her hip, or that her hand is half an inch too low during fouettés - you know, the 32 in a row straight kind.

My answer is always YES with a BIG SMILE and no further comment. I see it all. Of course, I see every little flaw of every level dancer. That is my job!! But...

I also see the potential and quality of a student's movement!! Because that is what ballet, dance, any athletic endeavor is... Movement.

Movement, not static poses that reflect rules of engagement, are the essence of every athletic endeavor, every Olympian. What ballet does is refine and create neural pathways that increase efficiency, strength, and stamina.

Potential vs. performance is a scale that tips back and forth during the training of any athlete, dancers very much included. But to decide and demand a perfect balance on a basic level is ludicrous.

A ballet student never leaves a skill level behind, but each advancing class level should build on skills learned previously like layers of a wedding cake!!

... And any advanced dancer knows that the hardest classes to take is basic!!

Support and encouragement are two mainstays of a person's development. Minute criticism and scrutiny is crushing. So...

Focus on the quality of movement. Encourage the crazy awkward steps to proficiency. Support yourself and your students by searching for glimpses of that balanced potential performance. If you are lucky, one day you may get to see it...

Perhaps onstage. But maybe in another sport, a college interview, a business presentation, or just when you go to the airport one holiday and see an adult student, son, or daughter walking toward you!

So... Let's never say you can't again! Okay?

Sometimes a student looks awesome on stage and really connects with the audience, but their technique may not be top notch. I would prefer a student like this any day!!

Skills can be improved, but that shine on stage is very difficult to "teach." Performance and potential aside, strength is still the foundation on which success rests.

Basic strength, especially in a female, is an important part of physical and mental health. It's what you stand on literally in the form of good strong legs and figuratively as in a healthy supportive self-image.

Guys tend to have more innate, built-in strength. Guys can usually jump higher, but my teacher expected the same jumping skills from females as well.

Female dancers were not exempt from any of the men's jumping exercises and benefitted by gaining strength which led to better pointe work and extension.

For our purposes, think of all ballet dancers as the perfect combination of marathon runner and sprinter.

Ballet trains the body to be ready for both possibilities; a long haul and a quick fast start.

Many classical variations, the little, short dances like *Nutcracker's* Sugar Plum, are... fifty seconds to a minute twenty seconds long. These are the equivalent of sprints in ballet.

Once the dancer starts, they dance nonstop till the end. The music is usually really fast or extremely slow, but make no mistake, the result is pure sprint.

The dancer goes from zero to 60 to catch the movement and perform the dance.

In contrast, *Giselle*, a two-act romantic ballet classic that any female dancer who aspires to be legend must perform, is almost two hours long. The female lead is onstage, and actively dancing about ninety nine percent of the time.

Giselle premiered in Paris on a Monday evening, June 28, 1841, with Carlotta Grisi as lead. She received immediate international acclaim for her interpretation of the title role of the peasant girl who dies when she is betrayed by love then rises from the grave to protect and defend her lover.

A first performance on a Monday night?

Wow!! These people had a lot of time on their hands...

Then consider a full length *Swan Lake*, the mother of all ballets, at three hours plus long.

The average time it takes regular type runners to do a marathon is between four and five hours, but the winning time in a major marathon ranges from 2:02 to 2:10 for men and 2:15 to 2:25 for women, less time than a full length *Swan Lake*.

Ballet encourages a "kick butt, fast out of the gates" strength but also requires the discipline and endurance of a "going the distance" marathon runner.

I can't think of many athletes other than dancers who train for both stamina and speed.

"Dancers are the athletes of God."
- Albert Einstein

Nobody likes to think about getting older, especially dancers, although the alternative really isn't that great!! If you develop the Strength and Stamina to be active as you age, then you might be lucky enough to have an opportunity to be the best person you can be for as long as possible.

An ability to be hardy and to hustle will certainly sustain your everyday life for years to come. Strength and Stamina are important. By contributing to your longevity and the value of your activities, the study of ballet correlates directly to the quality of the life that you live.

Now, when I say study ballet, what exactly am I talking about?

Go to class one time a week? Do I mean three times a week? Do I mean every day?

"When I miss class for one day, I know it. When I miss class for two days, my teacher knows it. When I miss class for three days, the audience knows it." -
Rudolf Nureyev

Professional dancers take way more than one class per day. They usually take two classes in the morning, a third in early afternoon and possible a fourth before diving into evening rehearsal.

Basically, dancers always moving. They're always dancing. They're always stretching, but even if you take one class a week, this will still help you.

So, my answer is... Please, take as many classes as you are able, but one class per week where you dance to your best optimal ability is far preferable than any number of classes per week that you "mark."

I've seen dancers dress for class and stretch before class. But during class, they "mark" the exercise with their hands or perform small minutia itty bitty parts of a step that is never really danced full out. This is a waste of time.

Dance every part of every class as if it is a performance. Full out. With as much energy and technique as you can muster.

Taking several classes a week is great, but it is most important to dance full out in the classes that you do take. Quality is as important as quantity.

As all we adults already know, life gets in the way sometimes. My best advice is, "If you tangle up, tango on." Been out of class a few weeks, months, years? Just go back as soon as you can, and be prepared to take a few Ibuprofen along the way.

Ballet is a life sport. It's not like getting on the balance beam; or dealing with the logistical details of riding a horse; or driving out to hike to the everlasting, then having to turn around and come back.

Ballet is efficient, effective, forgiving, and easily allows a student to initiate a do over.

Repeat! Ballet helps any endeavor you undertake.

Want to walk? Do some mountain biking? Ski? Go swimming? Ballet will support all those sports and more.

The three keys of ballet - posture, balance, and body alignment - give you viable tools that can easily expand for use in other activities.

Even if someone dances jazz, modern, or practices gymnastics or ice skating, he or she will almost always start off with some type of ballet barre, or a variation of a ballet barre when they begin their daily exercise routine.

They do this for an important reason.

Ballet is the most efficient foundation, podium, cornerstone, what-ever you want to call it, to foster excellence in any other type of dance or sports activity.

CHAPTER FOUR

COORDINATION

"Practice creates confidence. Confidence Empowers you." - Simone Biles

COORDINATION, defined as the ability to use different parts of the body smoothly and efficiently, allows the dancer to organize and connect necessary elements to produce effective movement.

An aptitude for coordination and communication between the dancer's mind and body enables Flexibility, Strength, Stamina, and Spatial Awareness to work together as a team.

I can hear you mumbling again! "Oh, but I've heard dancers are really uncoordinated when they're not dancing. In fact, I've heard that dancers are klutzes!!"

Every person is a total klutz at one time or another, but dancers as a species are very coordinated, and recognized for having a high degree of poise and composure.

"No dancer can watch Fred Astaire and not know that we all should have been in another business."
- Mikhail Baryshnikov

I use Baryshnikov quotes a little more than most because they are so insightful. I had the pleasure of taking class with Baryshnikov soon after he defected from the Soviet Union. In Russia, he was typecast as a character dancer, and thus not considered eligible to be invited to dance lead roles. Imagine that!

He had to defect, which means he disowned his allegiance to his home country and adopted the United States as his new home. That was a big deal, but he did this so he would have the freedom to dance the roles he obviously was born to dance.

In class and later backstage at the Municipal Auditorium in New Orleans, I had the opportunity not only to see Baryshnikov dance, but to interact with, and see how he treated other dancers. I was impressed by his generosity and deference. In class, he took his place in the last line, the traditional men's line, and waited patiently for his turn at the end of the line to perform exercises en diagonal. He was a gentleman. Kudos on all counts.

"Your character is your fate." – Maya Plisetskaya

Another quote from a famous Russian dancer. Ain't it the truth?

Many famous actors and actresses launched their professional career from a ballet studio: Patrick Swayze, Zoe Saldana, Charlize Theron, Neve Campbell, Sarah Jessica Parker, Penelope Cruz. And from Hollywood's Golden Age: Audrey Hepburn, Cyd Charisse, and Leslie Caron.

Channing Tatum studied ballet, jazz, and hip-hop in Cullman, AL.

After his early success in the first *Step-Up* movie, one of my young students at Huntsville Ballet who knew his grandmother made an impassioned plea to her to persuade him to come visit our class. He didn't, but I thought it was really sweet that the nine-year-old tried so hard!!

Whether at a dinner party, during college or employment interviews, or a first meeting, dancers present well. Their poised carriage inspires confidence, even to strangers. That reminds me of another adage: "You only have one chance to make a good impression."

I understand that people shouldn't judge a person based on first glance, and am the first to admit that when you get to know someone, first impression judgments may fly straight out the window.

Excuse me! I have seen *Pride and Prejudice* about a million times!! I know the dirty little secret that sometimes your first impression is completely wrong, but the fact remains that a favorable first impression can go a long way.

Initial impressions do make a difference. If you're stiff, cool, appear untouchable, and/or have no coordination or sense of movement, described in years past as possessing a certain grace, you are unable to project your best self.

But when you are coordinated, in control of your body because you know where you are in relations to objects and people surrounding you, because you possess the strength to stand there and meet someone head-on, then that's a win-win.

Coordination ties together all of the reasons that Ballet Helps Everything and will serve you well.

I confess that I am one lucky mom as well as ballet teacher. My own children and many of my students have placed in the top 20 of their high school graduating class. Each time I attend the ceremony, I observe other Top 20 recipients walk out on stage to stand, or take their seat, before they walk across the stage to receive their certificate of merit.

I cringe at their palpable discomfort and embarrassed pain. I've felt downright sorry for some of them, because they have absolutely no idea how to walk, or present in front of an audience.

Surprisingly, it doesn't seem to matter whether the student is a female in high heels, or a guy wearing regular "church" shoes that aren't the usual tennis shoes... although gaffs in high heels are usually quite spectacular.

I remember one poor girl who hooked her high heel in the hem of her long dress and split the seam straight up to her... yes, you guessed it.

No one bothers to rehearse these students. Many have no earthly idea of how to approach the podium, how to stand, or have any awareness of their posture, how to move, or even how to shake hands while holding a certificate or diploma.

Coordination is important throughout your life. There are beaucoup tasks that you will encounter in your life that are innately awkward. Grace and poise, supported by the coordination learned in ballet class, will smooth out the wrinkles.

Ponder the potentials.

Getting in and out of a canoe, ever tried that?

Coming down the stairs from a plane. You're not one of the Royals with a military officer standing and waiting to lend a hand. If you are one of the Royals, then please write a review for my book, Thank you very much.

What if you're wearing a backpack, holding a two year old by the hand, and trying to grip the railing? Believe it or not, I've been on some planes recently, where deplaning still occurs on steep steps or high ramps. Pretty hard to accomplish!!

If you're not able to coordinate or control your body, these physical tasks will be complicated and, worst case scenario, might not even be doable.

And these are just the coordination of physical demands.

What about mental tasks that require focus and coordination? Cooking dinner. Doing homework. Studying for a test. Deciding on a budget and paying bills. Evaluating if your co-worker is a real friend. Deciphering what exactly your boyfriend or mom or sister meant by what they just said...

These little normal occurrences might be easier if you lived a more coordinated existence through controlled movement and mindful thought. The pattern of your life is a kind of dance in itself, and may have a chance of being better, smoother, and more enjoyable.

Ballet matches movement to music. The combination of steps and choreography requires a coordinated effort of mind and body before any dance can begin. That specialized training offers a tenfold payback for you, your body, your life.

"The expression should come from within oneself conveying the spiritual - Something between earth and Heaven. And if one runs, one should not seem to touch the ground."
- Natalia Makarova

CHAPTER FIVE

DYNAMIC ENERGY

"What are you waiting for? What are you saving for? Now is all there is." -
George Balanchine

DOES the thought of Dynamic Energy make you tired? Guess that's
one way to look at it but... I challenge you to examine the concept...
and the alternative.

Dynamic Energy is marked by continuous, productive activity, or
applies to a change marked by forceful energy. Another two-fold definition. Dynamic energy can refer to a dynamic personality or relate to a
physical force or energy.

Now think about how difficult it would be to accomplish the tasks
of the day without a good dose of dynamic energy. That to me is a far
worse proposition. Exhausting...

A person's attitude projects long before a single word is uttered.

Consider the dynamic energy you communicate when you meet someone, when you plan or perform a task at home, work, or school.

Many times, you observe people who may get the job done, but they drag their "you know what" the entire time. They hardly move and seem to operate in slow motion.

Okay, we all have seen people like this, or perhaps have even been this person. You can conjure the vivid picture in any number of job positions, where you're like, "Seriously, can't you just kind of get in gear?"

Let's face it, as a person, it is imperative to "get in gear" to be able to actually complete an assignment. You can't laze your way through anything and expect good results.

How does studying ballet shape dynamic movement? By cultivating a palpable energy that makes a person more appealing and more accomplished.

The dynamic energy somebody projects when they enter a room makes a difference.

In all executive presence classes for major corporations, the first thing that the presenter works on is posture and keeping your balance between your feet, followed by hand movements and gestures. Ask Jeff over at Amazon!

I have seen so many dancers, male and female, go onstage to perform a variation that I can tell, almost from the first step from the wings, whether the variation will be a success or... not.

Does the dancer slouch as they run onstage? Do they drag their feet? Readjust their opening position? Look anywhere but at their audience? Take their position incrementally, feet first, then core body, then arms? Are they smiling?

You might be thinking, "Oh, God, she's talking about posture. My mother told me stuff like this." If she did, good for her, but I'm discussing more than posture, I'm talking presence and economy of motion.

Presence generates confidence, and sparks the attention of your target audience.

Economy of motion protects the energy you do have by using it sparingly, and only when it will assist in accomplishing the goal. A lot of energy is expended when a person drags their feet and slouches their shoulders. There we go, back to the posture thing.

And you are right, your body does use dynamic energy to control your posture and really stand up straight to stay on balance, but energy is expended either way. And the results of doing it right?

Ahh, the results are stunning.

The study of ballet helps a student increase the energy and resolve necessary to correct posture, develop strength, muscle memory, and care for the body that you're given.

Let's face it, we live in one, single body, and somehow, we must come to terms with that body. Many teachers say that a dancer's body is their instrument.

Tru Dat! Ballet is the best way to nurture the body you are born with.

Ballet supports the mindset and attitude with which you approach your body. It's a partnership. The mind and body have a direct relationship with each other.

One supports the other.

The confidence and good self-image that comes from excellent posture, strength, flexibility, balance, coordination, body alignment, and spatial awareness combines to form a winning combination.

Dynamic energy can first encourage, and then propel, students into believing that they can do what they set their minds to, whether it's dance a step or complete a task. "Yes, I am able to do this and if not, I will try until I do." This is an important mindset that can be very helpful in whatever you do, whether you're a doc, a nurse, a lawyer... Or an older dancer.

Ballet is a lifelong avocation. Dancers often continue to take class for many years beyond their performing career. My teacher had many former students who continued to take advanced class with us, long after their professional careers were over.

There were two sisters that I remember well. Both were Radio City Music Hall Rockettes in the heyday!

This was a high honor!

The original standards to become a Rockette were incredibly stringent and difficult to maintain, but both the sisters won a spot and had long dance careers. I met them years later, long after their retirement.

The sisters had platinum, aka Marilyn Monroe, hair and both wore stage makeup to class. They dressed in the appropriate attire, although their mid-length hair was not pulled back into a bun. They were the only dancers to ever not wear a bun to Miss Haller's class.

They took discreet places at the barre, and I remember they wore soft black ballet shoes, which were a bit out of place, since all the female dancers in the advanced class never wore ballet shoes again once they graduated to pointe shoes.

We would wear worn out pointe shoes for barre through petit allegro in the center, then change to newer pointe shoes for the last half of the class. The reason behind this was a simple one: We never wore soft ballet shoes on stage so why practice in them?

Back to the Sistas! These Ladies never really spoke to us or Miss Haller, but during class they would sometimes smile, giggle, and pass a word or two between themselves, almost as if they were twins with a secret language.

Miss Haller never gave them corrections or advice. In fact, she acted as if they were not even there. She tolerated their presence but did not condone it. The Sisters would attend Saturday class, which began at twelve noon and ran a full two hours.

The dancers in the class would treat them much the same. Their technique at barre was okay, but some of their centre work was a bit laughable, especially jumps and beats.

Generally, we concentrated on our own mistakes and corrections, and viewed their efforts as amusing, as long as they didn't get in our way... which they didn't.

But there was one thing that the Sistas did to ensure that they were welcome anytime.

They brought a plate of homemade cookies whenever they attended class.

When they arrived, they would place the cookies on top of an old Victrola cabinet set in the corner where Miss Haller stood.

The Sistas would curtsy to Miss Haller, and with a grand gesture, place the plate of cookies on the top of the old brown wooden cabinet as an offering to the god of the class.

We as dancers knew perfectly well that Miss Haller would never touch the cookies.

She would wait until after the last rehearsal of Saturday afternoon before proclaiming that it would be a shame to waste food.

That was the signal!

All the dancers still standing would descend and take a single cookie from the offering. Delish! Wonderful!

The cookies were a pay to play gesture from the Sistas. A welcomed, generous gift.

Many years later, I learned that one of the Sistas had passed. A group of us went to the funeral at Schoen's on Canal Street. Sure enough, she was buried along with her platinum hair and full stage make up, in one of her Rockettes costumes.

She was over one hundred years old. When the Sistas danced with us, they were in their mid-seventies. We didn't have a clue. Their technique seems golden to me now!

What is the point to my story? Ballet dancers always have a home in the studio. Since ballet is a universal culture, dancers can take class and immediately find a group of friends in any city or country they live in. Awesome!

CHAPTER SIX

MUSICALITY AND RHYTHM

"When a body moves, it's the most revealing thing. Dance for me a minute, and I'll tell you who you are." - Mikhail Baryshnikov

ALTHOUGH BALLET IS AN ATHLETIC ENDEAVOR, ballet is also an art. Dancing to music, or at the very least, dancing to a rhythmic beat that can be fully translated as music, elevates the study of ballet to a cultural art form.

Expressions such as "dancing to the beat of your own drum," "dancing to the rhythm of your heart," and "life taps its toes to your beat," reflect the individuality of a person's movement. A person exhibits musicality and rhythm every time they make a step. Think of Yul Brenner walking... What a sight!

Now, I know what's flipping around in your head. You're thinking, "Gee, I took some dance classes before my daughter's wedding, or when I was my best friend's maid of honor." Yes, that probably helped you through a very public social situation, but even a few social dance lessons would be so much easier if you have some prior ballet training.

If you listen to music, you may have an appreciation how music creates a harmony in our lives. There's a rhythm, and a certain melody to everything in our lives: the wind in the trees, the chimes waving in the breeze on your front porch, and yes, just in the way somebody moves. This serves as an introduction to the music of the ballet.

"See the music, hear the dance."
- George Balanchine

Ballet music is not strictly about counting the number of beats in a phrase, but also, about interpreting the steps, within the boundaries that those beats and phrasing suggest.

The music is the chord that brings the dancers and choreography together. The beat of the music that is rehearsed over and over can, and I've experienced this personally during a performance, keep everyone dancing even in the event of a music malfunction or outage.

Have you ever seen the dancers just continue dancing?

There's even one ballet that doesn't allow the dancers to hear the fully realized, orchestrated music until they dance the choreography on opening night, in order to purposefully elicit a different, and perhaps totally new and fresh perspective.

A dancer's interpretation of the music through the choreography offers a picture into the soul of a dancer. Where do they pause? Are the steps emphasized? Where? Is the extension held for a period of time?

Varying speeds allow for individual style that may support a longer balance, or extra airtime during jumps. How a dancer moves, and the rhythm that they move with, is as personal as a signature.

That is the reason an audience returns, fascinated and expectant, when a new Prima Ballerina is chosen to dance a well-worn and much seen role. Each person who dances the lead role is unique and individual.

I've seen *Giselle* and *Swan Lake* many times, and each performance is different because each lead dancer interprets the choreography and music in their own special way. Wonderful!

Some dancers move well to a very slow rhythm, and if that's their understanding of the role and music, then respect their performance. You can appreciate a person's beat if it is real and true. Some people dance better to a faster rhythm.

The more you understand music, the more you will value the movement within the music. When a student takes ballet class, they learn how to accomplish and abide with the pace of the steps within the music.

The music a teacher uses in class is very telling and as individual as a performer's version of a role. The music should be consistent and complex, not just a banging on the piano keys of rhythm.

I know teachers who use Broadway show music, themes from movie soundtracks, and even popular music.

I use classic ballet music, but I am particular about my pianists. Mr. Whitt at Huntsville Ballet was great. He would design the class music around different themes and mix it up. "Diamonds are a Girl's Best Friend" always brought a smile.

Miss Haller used the same music in every class, varying the music for centre work, but always within the confines of classical. She actually commissioned a group of musicians to play the music she wanted to use, then had records made from the recording... This was a long time ago when she founded the school.

What I don't like is someone who uses trash music that is only chosen for a beat. My sister and I met at a "dance convention" once, big mistake. The "master class" teacher, and I use the term loosely, played "Turkey in the Straw" for the entire class. Worst class ever!

Enjoy your music, but have it planned out and organized ahead of time! Best Advice ever!

CHAPTER SEVEN

BODY ARTICULATION

"The higher up you go, the more mistakes you are allowed. Right at the top, if you make enough of them, it's considered to be your style."
- Fred Astaire

BODY ARTICULATION REFERS to the place at which two joints are linked or united, either rigidly, or in such a way as to permit motion, within the body. The body articulates at this juncture.

So, strictly speaking, body articulation is about how the different joints in your body move. Your knee and elbow are hinge joints. Your shoulder and hip are ball and socket joints. Each has their own defined range of motion.

In ballet, articulations are also a way of expressing precision and control over your own body.

There is a relation between articulation and spatial awareness, but body articulation gets even more specific in terms of range of motion. How do your joints move? How far can your joints move? What is their range of motion?

A dog's tail does not wag the dog. The dog wags the tail.

Ideally... I knew a boxer once that acted like his tail was in charge! But...

A dancer should move from the inside out. When arms take any position in the repertoire, the movement should initiate from the center core, then through the muscles of the shoulder to the arm to move elbows, wrists, then fingers.

There is a famous solo called *"The Dying Swan,"* not really one of my favorites because it consists of a lot of bourres and angst. However, the dance really revolves around the movement of the dancer's arms, which are a perfect example of body articulation.

Watch the movement as it fully articulates from the core to the shoulders then the elbows, wrists, and fingers. The arms are exquisite. That is why the dance is a classic.

The combination of range of motion and flexibility in any joint equals the articulation of that joint in your body. Articulation intensifies the control you have over your body.

Your body has many different kinds of joints: hinge joints like the knee and elbow, ball and socket joints like the hip and shoulder.

Ballet teaches all the possible movements capable in each joint. Which way does it move? How far? Do you turn out or turn in from the hip? How do you stand on your feet? Do your feet roll in? Do they roll out? Do your knees knock together? Are you bowlegged? A ballet studio is full of mirrors and they are there for a reason. Take a good long look!!

Ballet training teaches you to examine how your body moves. How your joints articulate contributes to your ability to execute any given task, whether it be a ballet step, or a sports or exercise activity.

If the range of motion of your joints is limited, then the movement of those joints is reduced.

Limited articulation of your joints directly impacts longevity and quality of life. Some people can't turn their head very well from side to side. Some can't even lift their head.

By increasing flexibility and expanding the range of motion in all of your joints, you will move better, and possibly live longer. Range of motion improves more than performance in ballet and sports. Increased body articulation improves life!!

CHAPTER EIGHT

TECHNICAL SKILL AND EFFORT

"I do not try to dance better than anyone else. I only try to dance better than myself."
- Mikhail Baryshnikov

WHY PAIR technical skill with effort? Because greater technical skill, the ability to actually dance the steps, is directly affected by the effort you put into your class. I always ask my students, "Do you take class? Or do you dance class?" There is a big difference.

I will use cellphones as a perfect example. If a friend is talking face to face with you about a problem at home or an agenda at a meeting, whatever. Or if a child is trying to speak with a parent about a situation at school. Is that friend or parent really listening if they are looking, or even considering taking a look, at their cellphone?

The answer is no. Not in the least.

Their attention is diverted and scattered. Can they hope to understand what is being said by their friend or child if they are not listening?

Technical skill demands effort.

A dancer not only listens to corrections but must apply those corrections to steps that their body is attempting to dance. Understanding is involved. Awareness and observation of other dancers' strengths and weaknesses may help you accomplish a step in a more efficient, artistic manner. Consistent effort will heighten technical skill.

Completing ballet steps and combinations is a pure technical skill that increases the ability of your body to be mindful and attentive to detail and surroundings. .

The increased consciousness of how others move translates into a better knowledge of how you can move.

You may counter with, "Oh well, but I'm never going to be good at ballet. I started when I was 30. I started when I was 40."

Age and body type don't matter. This is personal. You can always go back and pick up some help or tips from a good ballet class. Ballet will always allow you to move better, faster, slower, and with more grace.

The exercises help you keep moving, while building your strength and stamina.

All that adds up to technical skill, and the importance of technical skill in adding quality to life's day-to-day environment cannot be undervalued.

Technical skill is not an enemy. Competence and the standard of excellence should be a goal of any endeavor.

What do I mean by this?

One thing that makes me crazy... Only one thing?

I know parents who send their student to a school that offers less rigorous, inferior quality dance education with the reasoning that it is "more fun."

This, I do not understand. I cannot comprehend.

Would those parents send their student to a school that taught substandard

Math or incorrect English because everyone is allowed to goof around and do whatever they want during class?

I don't think so... And ballet education is no different.

I have great fun in all my classes. I use hula hoops to teach stability of arms in first position during chaine turns. I bring basketballs in to teach the physics of jumping. I have my students "bounce or dribble" a partner on the head as if they are basketballs. Why? If the student who is jumping is rebounding correctly off the floor, the feel of a dribbling basketball will be perfectly reproduced.

I use seasonal music and show music. I pace the class, so we are always moving from one exercise to the next. I tell stories and my students dance.

Ballet is an intrinsic skill, one that brings pleasure, competence, and confidence to the student. Look for a class that is well controlled with minimal talking, moves quickly with a maximum of one third of the class spent at the barre. Look for technical skill that comes from within the competence of the teacher. Look for the smiles!

CHAPTER NINE

THE CONCENTRATION AND FOCUS OF DISCIPLINE

"Plie is the first thing you learn and the last thing you master." - Suzanne Farrell

WHAT ULTIMATELY CONTROLS YOUR BODY? Your mind.

How you think determines your attitude, ability, and even your success.

Ballet develops a dancer's concentration and focus to form a habit of discipline, in particular self-discipline.

Concentration, focus and discipline are signposts on the roadmap of ballet.

"God gives talent. Work transforms talent into Genius." - Anna Pavlova

. . .

Discipline's gotten a bad rap in recent years. A lot of people don't even like to talk about discipline, because they immediately associate discipline with corporal punishment, which is absurd. That has nothing to do with the discipline I'm talking about.

When I think of discipline, I think of precision, persistence, and the ability to perform. These are talents that are important to us as people. There is a proficiency that I want to nurture, whether I'm talking about ballet, loyalty to family, or a task well done.

By incorporating discipline as an essential ingredient of character, a student will cultivate the will to stick to their commitments, to keep working at a task, and to see it through to completion.

A student who learns self-discipline will be better able to choose wisely and discern worthwhile activities and pursuits. They won't just quit and give up.

As a student's technical skill improves, so does the concentration and focus necessary to advance to the next class level. A student can start out with a very minimal plié, which is bending the knees in one of the five basic positions. Knees should bend directly over your big toe, no more, no less. What if a student can't get their knees directly over their big toe? Work with what you have!

Keep trying! Don't give up!

Work a little at a time until that goal is achieved. I've had many students eventually "find" their plies, but I also remember the frustration with their first attempts at the step. As discussed earlier, a student can logically understand what I want them to do, and still not be able to make their body do it.

So... Ballet is progressive and incremental.

Success comes from constant repetition and correction.

Love your corrections. This shows that the teacher is concerned and attentive to your efforts.

Each skill builds onto the one before. The first five positions are the base from which to begin movement. The five steps presented in basic class form the foundation of Petit Allegro – Glissade, Assemble,

Jete, Ballonné, and Pas de Basque. Learning these early steps bring the basic student to the threshold of combinations.

Intermediate class solidifies combinations and introduces diagonal work including turns and Grand Allegro (Big Jumps) as well as pointe work. As the body learns the steps, the mind matures and grows. Concentration and focus produce the discipline it takes to persevere. All a little at a time, in order and harmony.

Class is very "in the moment."

A student should only be thinking and working on the skill presented in the step at that single moment in time. Perform the exercise as best you can and go from there.

Expecting too much too soon only leads to disappointment. Remember the Pre-Ballet parents?

Most professional dancers will tell you that they are never satisfied with a performance, no matter how their audience raves. They speak the truth. If a dancer is really good, they are always trying to improve. Yes, when this dissatisfaction turns into an elusive search for perfection, that can be a bad thing, a warning sign.

But use the dream of perfection to achieve the goal of excellence.

"Perfection is not attainable, but if we chase perfection, we can catch excellence."
- Vince Lombardi

Don't ever confuse the word discipline with perfection.

One of the bad raps that ballet often gets is it teaches a person to crave perfection. I will not argue that ballet does not hold high standards, especially at a professional level.

During class and rehearsal, I've seen teachers argue whether a student's hand is half an inch too low, or too high while doing fouettés. I've seen knock-down-drag-outs about whether hands should be directly above the head in fifth position port de bras or slightly in front of the head.

All kinds of little things... Whether a student was hiking their shoulder up. Whether hands should be in first, pulled in, or en bas during pirouettes. Would it be better if arms were slightly higher, if elbows were more rounded?

These are all fine points that can and are examined, and often precipitate a lively discussion. View these discussions as perseverance talking, not a quest for perfection.

Children dance all the time — around the house, in the yard, and up grocery store aisles – and dance lessons might refine and direct their boundless energy.

Once, on my way to deliver the lunch count to the school office, the long hall before me proved too tempting! I started performing big jumps between the doors of the classrooms, of course. I think I was in second grade. When the principal stopped me and asked what I was doing, I answered, "Grand jetés." She smiled and sent me on my way. Whew! That was close!

But before you take your promising dancer to the first class, there is an important caveat that you should commit too. Do not expect your free spirit to immediately love the discipline and work that will be demanded.

The etiquette of the ballet class is centuries old and an essential ingredient of the "training" process that your child will benefit from. Take a forward view and believe that truth that you are teaching your child a lifelong skill that is an important and worthy undertaking.

Commit for the entire school year, and let the child know that the yearlong commitment is the plan. You are the adult and there is no room for argument. Make this is an agreement between you, who prepares and brings your child to class, and the child who participates as the dancer.

Which leads to the most important aspect of starting class... Attendance.

A student must attend class regularly to get anything out of the instruction. Once or twice a month just won't do it. Is the result worth it? Absolutely, but you must get yourself or your student to the studio. Class must be taken.

Sounds like a foregone conclusion. Right?

Not so. If a child is not present on a regular basis, the instruction will not take root.

And attendance also implies that the student is rested and prepared, as in proper attire, hair up in a bun, and ready to go.

Remember that your time and money will only be well spent if the student fully engages in the lessons paid for.

Dancers don't give up. Not in class. Not in performance. And certainly not in life.

Perseverance is the quality that combines strength and stamina into endurance. The will to continue is born from the discipline of attending class and working within the confines of your body to excel.

Whether you are an advanced dancer or an aspiring one, perseverance should be the goal that dances with you.

"Don't be afraid to be amazing. "
- Andy Offutt Irwin

I would like to say that I see students who give their one hundred percent every day, but what I often see is a terrible sense of timidity. A reluctance to really dig deep and go for the higher jump, the greater number of turns.

Many are content with acceptance rather than achievement. I want to see boldness. I don't care if you get it wrong. I want to see you give it a go and try your best. Then... I want to see the exercise again.

I want you to dance.

Perseverance is the virtue that gets you through tough difficult times. Whether in class or out. Work your best and all your potential will be exhibited in your performance. No doubt!!

Remember... When Mother Theresa was asked what she prayed for... she said, "Final Perseverance." That's my plan. Make it yours.

Make it so!! Ready?

. . .

The concept of incremental progression should be instilled in every student, because the idea of getting better a little at a time can help the student understand the mind-body connection necessary to master steps and combinations.

A mind-body link is encouraged by the study of ballet.

I often ask my students to mentally picture themselves performing a particularly difficult step or series of steps... Like fouettés or a wonderful extension of the leg.

Sometimes this exercise generates break throughs. The mind and body click! The result is the ability to perform the step!

Concentration improved by ballet class can translate easily to long term goals. Improved memory and cognitive association make intellectual tasks easier to learn and perform.

Whether school, home, or office, if a person can connect the dots of different concepts easily and with understanding, their performance will improve.

The ability to direct your body to do what your brain wants it to do is a huge and even freeing proposition. How many people can do that? Not too many.

If you're a ballet parent, you will notice improved timing and absorption in your student's studies at school. Ballet helps studies at school.

In fact, I cannot think of one student in my 40+ years of teaching who was a terrible student in school, unless they just were intentionally sabotaging themselves, which is a whole other story.

Usually, ballet dancers are extremely smart, and often rise to top academic levels, even considering the time they spend in class and rehearsal.

The classes teach time management skills and organization. If a student learns to focus and concentrate, then that student has also mastered discipline which makes quite a lot possible.

When I studied with Miss Haller, she was quite strict, as were most of the teachers in her era, about sticking with your single teacher. She taught the classic Bourneville style, for which I am eternally grateful, with emphasis on fast, clean Petite Allegro and wonderful Grande Allegro.

She expected loyalty. I once heard her complain that her students were corrupted because they went over the summer to study at American Ballet Theatre with Danilova!!

This is just not the norm anymore. Dancers today must be more flexible as they will usually train in diverse styles and techniques of ballet.

Many times, a student will be asked to perform a step whether it be pirouettes, jumps, développés, several different ways during their career.

They will usually work with several teachers before they find which style works best for them and their body type. Most of us do not live in Russia!

As students of ballet, we have the opportunity to observe schools of ballet education and experience many styles of teaching.

Dancers are expected to be adaptable. During a dancer's course of study, they may be exposed to several ballet syllabi – Vaganova, Cecchetti, Royal Academy of Dance, the French School, Balanchine (School of American Ballet), and Bournonville.

But every one of these ballet curricula will teach the concentration and focus necessary to establish a discipline that reaches for excellence, not perfection. Trying to be better. Pressing to move forward and keep working.

That's a discipline I can live with because it fosters a willpower that's essential to succeed in any endeavor in our lives.

CHAPTER TEN

CULTURAL ENRICHMENT

"Play the last measure very softly."
- Anna Pavlova

BALLET AS AN ART form is an integral part of our cumulative artistic treasure yet also possesses a rich culture all its own. The manners preserved by classroom etiquette and the common language of standardized French terminology ensure that ballet embraces a truly global philosophy.

A student can take class in a studio located in any part of the world and the familiar mores will be recognizable.

Evolving from Italian court dances in the fifteenth century, ballet terminology and steps were first formalized during the reign of Louis IX, Le Roi Soleil.

As ballet was imported to the courts of the Russian Czars, ballet developed some of the most enduring music and choreography ever performed.

Ballet exposes students to timeless beauty.

How many other sports or activities can make that claim?

The choreography, music, pageantry, pantomime, the eternal themes of the ballet represent the best of humanity.

Women have always been on top in ballet. Growing up, I felt like men were props, because ballet is very much a female endeavor. I always like to see a good male dancer, and it is extremely fascinating to watch someone who's really good, tremendously rewarding. I remember Baryshnikov then and immediately think of Sergei Polunin now. But...

Ballet is about the ballerina. Ballet is about the female. Males in ballet are there to support their partner, to watch their partner. They're there to honor their partner. Mr. B seems to agree...

"In my ballets, woman is first. Men are consorts. God made men to sing the praises of women. They are not equal to men: They are better." - George Balanchine

And the themes of the classic Ballets are immortal, *Swan Lake, Sleeping Beauty, Les Sylphides, and Giselle.* The big theme that is common to all ballet is love, the timeless, enduring love that transcends even death.

When I think of *Giselle,* I especially think of the related themes of betrayal and forgiveness. These are important themes that speak to our humanity.

Adolphe Adam wrote the music for *Giselle*; this was the only ballet music the guy ever wrote. I mean, figure that, the only ballet he ever wrote, and *Giselle* remains the perfect endearing example of a romantic classical ballet.

Giselle is not only still performed, but revered as the benchmark for dancers, male or female, to dance.

Dance all the *Swan Lakes* you want, whatever. *Swan Lake* may be next in line as an epitome, but as a dancer, if you have not danced *Giselle*, then you have not really reached the pinnacle of your career.

Ballet offers beauty, culture, the best of humanity free for the taking. There is just a certain breathlessness to a great ballet performance.

If you've ever seen *Giselle*, or *Swan Lake*, or just two people dancing a simple beautiful pas de deux, then you have seen magic. Total magic.

Ballet does help everything, including our spirit, because once you are exposed to magic, you are indelibly marked with an understanding that is beyond comprehension.

"Genius is another word for magic, and the whole point of magic is that it is inexplicable."
- Margot Fonteyn

Not everyone who takes ballet will be a professional dancer. In fact, only a fraction of 1% of all students may become a professional dancer. As a teacher and a mother, I'm not even sure that buying into that lofty goal is a great idea.

Professional dancers don't get paid very much, unless they are at the absolute at the top of their game, employed by a big company, seen by the right people, and a whole host of other things that have to do with luck, politics, and other variables that they have no control over.

I've witnessed American Ballet Theatre company dancers exit the studios in a dreadful hurry to get to their supplemental job as a hostess or wait staff at a restaurant.

The regular Corps de Ballet are not working for the money. Later on, as they end their professional careers, they may get paid to teach or tour with other companies, but the life of a dancer is not something that's going to make you rich.

Not with money... But ballet will make you rich in terms of how you present yourself, how you live your life!

If ballet does nothing more than solidify your posture, balance, and body alignment, the three keys to ballet, I'll be happy, and you'll be better off... And you'll be able to translate your skills and adequately participate in almost any sport endeavor.

You'll have a grasp of spatial awareness, where you are in relation to your environment, other people and things moving in your environment. Flexibility, in muscles, joints, tendons, will allow you to lead a quality life, and maintain your independence as you age.

The stronger you become, the more you'll be able to accomplish, and you'll be better able to recover from any life accidents.

Life throws a lot of curve balls that will require strength to deal with, not only physical vigor, but a firm mental ability that helps you persevere, that helps keep you going.

Coordination of mind, body and movement will allow you to present your best as a person. You will have to interact and "perform" in the world unless you plan on becoming a hermit or something.

You'll find yourself meeting different people in unfamiliar situations. Coordination of your talents will help you make sense of those situations and achieve better results in your family, school, or career.

Through the study of ballet, the dynamics of your movement will improve. You'll have a lot more energy. Elevated musicality and rhythm increase a sense of happiness and well-being, in a better tuned way.

Your body articulation, the precision and control you have over your body, can work wonders for a person's appearance. Let's face it, if you look in the mirror and like what you see, you'll feel a little better.

Technical skill and focus blend, then connect your body to your mind, and that mind-body click manifests in your attitude.

How your mind perceives people, things, and situations becomes a reflection of your world view and philosophy of life.

The ability to concentrate and complete a task within standards of excellence will set you apart from the crowd.

Perseverance if you don't understand, or if you're learning something new, will mark you as someone that is easy and fulfilling to work with.

When you possess the discipline to complete an undertaking, then your self-confidence will be bolstered by self-reliance.

Finally, the beauty and culture of the art form of ballet enriches your life beyond physical boundaries. I've seen older dancers, who for one reason or another are wheelchair-ridden, but they still get so such enjoyment and thrill from seeing a ballet, listening to the music, and even observing class.

Ballet is a life skill. Class will forever beckon. Once you're a dancer, you're always a dancer. If you move to different cities, go to a ballet school. You'll have an instant in. You'll find friends quickly. Friend me!

Ballet really does help everything. I think it's great, and I hope that you have the opportunity to study at a decent school.

In other booklets, I will detail the Three Keys of Ballet and relate how to apply these principles. I'll examine qualities to look for in a good studio, ballet class, and teacher.

If you're a teacher, I'll discuss a plan for a Pre-Ballet program that builds a foolproof pyramid system. When you begin with excellent classes for young pre-ballet dancers, the results expand all the way up to your advanced class.

I'll discuss ways to keep those students, lessen attrition, and develop your best product, because let's face it, your advanced students are the culmination of your work. They are the ultimate product that you're trying to produce.

If you're the parent of a student, I'll compare different methods of teaching ballet, the dance climate in the United States, and how to get the best out of ballet instruction.

"The one important thing I have learned over the years is the difference between taking one's work seriously and taking one's self seriously. The first is imperative and the second is disastrous."
- Margot Fonteyn

Ballet is an important part of my life, but ballet is not my entire life. Ballet is something I've always done, but ballet is not my complete identity.

In addition to taking classes, then teaching classes, I've also found immeasurable happiness in my family, children, and my writing. I'm an excellent lap swimmer and last year, I took to the snow slopes for the first time in my entire life.

I was never just a dancer. My identity and the identity of your student, yourself should travel far beyond the walls of the studio and theatre.

I had the pleasure of meeting Margot Fonteyn after a performance of Giselle in the Municipal Auditorium in New Orleans. I was a young dancer, just having entered the advanced class at age fifteen.

My two friends and I were ushers for the performance, which meant that we could squeeze into the lighting box to watch the performance after our ushering job was complete. This was the way we could attend multiple performances and not have to pay for tickets.

We knew the ins and outs of the Municipal Auditorium because we had danced there many times for Mardi Gras balls, the Opera, and in recitals, so we decided to sneak backstage.

Our stated goal was to see Rudolph Nureyev who had just defected from the Soviet Union. We just wanted a glimpse. He was young, handsome, and he brought a new energy to the role of Albrecht. We thought his dancing was wonderful.

This was something akin to sneaking backstage to see the Beatles.

Nureyev and Dame Margot Fonteyn were considered the most dynamic adagio pair at the time, which was a little odd since he was so much younger. But they possessed a chemistry that is the mainstay of all famous adagio pairs. Just something special between the two of them.

Well, security was pretty tight because they expected crowds of screaming girls, like with the Beatles, to try to get to see Nureyev.

Suddenly, my friends and I saw two guards marching toward us. Guess we didn't blend in as well as we thought.

We panicked and immediately ducked into the nearest room to hide and wait for the guards to pass us by.

We didn't look at the name on the door. We were scared and we waltzed straight into...

Dame Margot Fonteyn's dressing room.

The Royal Ballet Prima could have reacted. She would have been totally justified in calling security to escort us out. She could have yelled and screamed at the girls who disturbed her rest after an evening of work.

Instead, she welcomed us.

The older woman with the slight, even frail physique, was gracious and generous with three young dancers who made a mistake.

She smiled and invited us to have a cup of tea with her.

We sat and talked. We asked her about ballet and her life and her hot partner. She took her time to speak with us... No rush, just a perfectly leisurely visit, as if she had invited us long ago... All this after just dancing a high power and incredibly memorable performance of Giselle.

Dame Margot Fonteyn was a real Lady, a role model for the ages.

I hope you have enjoyed this discussion. The study of ballet offers a rich life. I've seen it over and over. Ballet really does help everything, especially everything that is not ballet.

AFTERWORD

Thank you for reading *Ballet Helps Everything! - Ten Reasons Why*, the first book in the Garage Ballet series.

If you liked the book and would be willing to spare a minute, please share a review on Amazon.

You can also post the same review to my author page on Goodreads –

https://www.goodreads.com/dawncrouch

Many Thanks!

ABOUT THE AUTHOR

A native of New Orleans, Dawn C Crouch is a former dancer with Houston Ballet under the direction of James Clouser and Nicholas Polejenko. She holds a degree in political science, earned at the University of Houston.

She pursued a graduate and has written copy for a living, all while continuing to teach at ballet studios throughout the southeast.

Ballet is a small world and Dawn enjoys many connections with former colleagues, personal friends and past students who work in major ballet companies throughout the United States and Europe. She has directed and danced in numerous ballet productions and possesses a true passion for her subject.

BALLET HELPS EVERYTHING! is the premiere book of GARAGE BALLET, a popular series of nonfiction instructional booklets that detail her experience and life as both a dancer and teacher. Please visit Garageballet.com for updates and new titles.

ALSO BY DAWN C CROUCH

Pointe Work - Ten Reasons Why and When

The ABCs of PreBallet - The Essential Building Block

Against The Wind - Jane-Claire's Personal Salvation

The Last Plague

Made in the USA
Las Vegas, NV
30 April 2021

22278505R00049